MED

ATHLETES

MEDITATIONS FOR ATHLETES

Bob Sessoms

Illustrated by Jon R. Sessoms

ABINGDON PRESS
NASHVILLE

MEDITATIONS FOR ATHLETES

Library of Congress Cataloging-in-Publication Data

SESSOMS, BOB
    Meditations for athletes.
    1. Sports—Moral ethical aspects. 2. Sports—Religious
    aspects—Christianity. I. Title.
GV706.3.S47   1987   175   87-12552

ISBN 0-687-24128-6 (alk. paper)

This book is printed on acid-free paper.

MANUFACTURED BY THE PARTHENON PRESS AT
NASHVILLE, TENNESSEE, UNITED STATES OF AMERICA

To
Frank Hart "Pogo" Smith—
a Christian friend and an example to
athletes and others

CONTENTS

PREFACE

"If you have ears, then, listen to what the Spirit says to the churches! To those who win the victory I will give some of the hidden manna. I will also give each of them a white stone on which is written a new name that no one knows except the one who receives it" (Revelation 2:17 TEV).

In biblical times a white stone symbolized several things. When casting lots or voting on a person's guilt or innocence, the white stone signified acquittal, not guilty, or forgiveness. A person who received freedom from slavery was given a white stone, symbolic of freedom. A soldier returning triumphantly from battle was presented with a white stone as a symbol of conquest over the enemy. Those who won athletic events often received white stones, symbolic of their victory.

As Christians, we are presented with "a white stone on which is written a new name." It is symbolic of God's salvation, of his forgiveness through his Son Jesus Christ, of our victorious life through Christ, and of our conquest over sin through Jesus. "To those who win the victory . . . I will also give each of them a white stone." As athletes, we win laurel wreaths, ribbons, banners, trophies; as Christian athletes, we will receive "a white stone on which is written a new name."

PRESEASON TRAINING FROM THE COACH

It is important to believe in yourself.

◇

Success Means Being Satisfied

Everyone cannot be the champ, the decathlon winner, the marathon runner, the subpar golfer, the All American, the M.V.P.

But we can succeed by doing our best, by giving 100 percent effort, by knowing we did our best, and by being satisfied because we did do our best.

The apostle Paul instructs us in this Christian concept:

> Let everyone be sure that he
> is doing his very best, for then
> he will have the personal satisfaction
> of work well done, and won't need
> to compare himself with someone
> else.   —Galatians 6:4 TLB

Too often we try to compare our athletic abilities with those of others, when in reality we need only compare our present performance with our past performance. We need to do our best, no matter what the outcome of the game. We may express disappointment, but if we did our best, we should be satisfied.

So it is with the Christian life: We need not compare ourselves with anyone else. We need only strive for perfection in the Christian way of life. Jesus should be our example to follow. As long as our relationship with him is in good order, our relationships with others will be right. When these relationships are proper, satisfaction and success become ours.

In athletics, we need to keep our relationships in proper perspective. No matter what position we play, our attitude toward God, ourselves, our parents, our coaches, our team members, our opponents, and the officials should be proper.

Then what is success? Jesus told a group of people: "You shall love the LORD your God with all your heart, with all your soul, and with all your mind. . . . You shall love your neighbor as yourself" (Matthew 22:37, 39 NKJV). By obeying these words of Jesus, we can succeed as athletes, as persons, as Christians.

You have only one life to live,
so make it the very best you
possibly can.

Your Talent

Your talent is an inheritance from God. Should someone die and leave you an inheritance, you would be very careful with it; so it should be with the inheritance you received from God—your talent.

To use your talent, you should neither bury it nor flaunt it (show off), but use it to God's glory.

God is not angry when you fail, but he expects you to do your best, to use the talent you have inherited. By using that talent, you are returning to God the gift (talent) he gave you.

"Christ has given each of us special abilities—whatever he wants us to have out of his rich storehouse of gifts" (Ephesians 4:7 TLB).

"You have a new life. It was not passed on to you from your parents, for the life they gave you will fade away. This new one will last forever, for it comes from Christ, God's ever-living Message to men" (I Peter 1:23 TLB).

Dear Pat:

As your parent I feel it is my privilege, as well as my obligation, to sit down and write you a letter. Today you tried out for your first athletic team, and I am proud of you. You made it! Making a team places you in a unique category—you are a team member. This carries with it much responsibility.

First, you have an obligation to yourself. You must now be willing to sacrifice those things you enjoy in order to train your body. That means eating the proper foods, getting adequate rest, and attending practice—and going over fundamentals until you are almost sick of them. It means disciplining yourself to keep up with your studies, even when you are dog-tired. It also means you must practice your Christianity more openly, but don't flaunt it. Keep reading the Bible and having prayer. It is so important that you set priorities so you can accomplish your goals as a Christian, as a student, and as an athlete.

Second, you have an obligation to your teammates. You are one part of a total team. Each member needs to do his or her part in order for the team to function at its best. Do not be selfish. This can kill a team's togetherness. Be glad when the others do well, and do your very best. Remember, just as the body of Christ has many parts and all are needed, so it is with a team. Do your best! Be the best part you can be.

As your Dad, I'll be cheering very hard for your team—and for you.

Love,
Your Dad

Words of Character

What is character? Character is found in people who have a distinctive quality of moral excellence. The following words describe a person with character:

STRONG:
One who possesses great resources.

TIRELESS:
One who has the capacity for endurance.

HONEST:
One who displays fairness and straightforwardness in conduct.

HUMBLE:
One who is not proud, haughty, or arrogant.

UNBENDING:
One who is unyielding in standing for right.

BRAVE:
One who shows courage and can endure trials.

DETERMINED:
One who is firm and resolute.
CHALLENGING:
One who has competitive interest and drive.
LOVING:
One who can show affection, compassion, and love.
MEEK:
One who can endure with patience and show no resentment.
LOYAL:
One who displays unselfish loyalty, concern, and admiration.
FAITHFUL:
One who is conscientious, steadfast, and demonstrates allegiance.
HOPEFUL:
One who has a genuine belief in fulfillment.
MERCIFUL:
One who shows compassion toward an offender.
PATIENT:
One who has the ability of forbearance.
GOOD:
One who is praiseworthy.
KIND:
One who is gentle and helpful.
SELF-CONTROLLED:
One whose own emotions are under control.
JOYFUL:
One who can rejoice and be happy.
STEADY:
One who is unfaltering, stable, not easily disturbed.

ENDURANCE

"When all kinds of trials and temptations crowd into your lives, my brothers, don't resent them as intruders, but welcome them as friends! Realise that they come to test your faith and to produce in you the quality of endurance" (James 1:2-3 Phillips).

Endurance! A word every athlete understands. It is the ability to endure that often separates the good athlete from the average.

Endurance comes through conditioning. It means running that extra lap or mile; it builds up the ability to outlast an opponent. All these words relate to endurance: *strength, patience, perseverance, steadfastness, courage, resistance*—and the athlete must possess all these to prepare for the testing of the game.

Can athletes possess all these qualities? They must, to produce, to give their best, to strive for the goal—victory. They must be in the best physical condition to endure the test of the game, to give their very best effort. Endurance helps the athlete put out that extra effort—to go all the way, to finish the race, to finish the game.

Just as the athlete needs to be in excellent physical condition in order to endure, the Christian must be in the best spiritual condition to endure the testing of the world. James writes to us about this endurance:

"Consider yourselves fortunate when all kinds of trials come your way, for you know that when your faith succeeds in facing such trials, the result is the ability to endure. Make sure that your endurance carries you all the way without failing, so that you may be perfect and complete, lacking nothing" (1:2-4 TEV).

There are times when the coach or a team member will test your faith. That's why you must endure spiritually. Read what prize you will win when you endure that testing of your faith:

"Happy is the person who remains faithful under trials, because when he succeeds in passing such a test, he will receive as his reward the life which God has promised to those who love him" (James 1:12 TEV). Or, as another translator states it: "Happy is the man who doesn't give in and do wrong when he is tempted, for afterwards he will get as his reward the crown of life that God has promised those who love him" (TLB).

How do we build up spiritual endurance? We must walk with the Lord daily—by studying the Bible, by memorizing Scripture, by praying, and by living our faith openly and unashamedly.

As training the body through exercise builds up physical endurance, to endure the trials of the world, Christians must train their spiritual bodies through knowledge of the Scriptures.

Our earthly coaches train us for a few brief years, doing their best for us, but God's training is always right and for our best good, that we may share his holiness. Training isn't enjoyable while it's happening—it hurts at times! But afterward we can see the result: a quiet growth in strength and endurance.

—HEBREWS 12:10-11 (Paraphrase)

Be Your Best

If the quarterback you cannot be,
  Be your best at the position you see.
If a tackle, a guard, or an end is your test—
  A back? a center? a kicker?—be your best!
If your skill lies on the court of basketball,
  Be your best, give the game your all.
If not a high scorer, put your mind at rest;
  As a defensive player—be your best.
If at bat you miss the ball,
  Be your best, no matter the call.
If on the bench you sit and rest,
  At practice, try harder—be your best.
If in track you come in last,
  Be your best; next time be fast!
If javelin, discus, or pole vault is your test,
  Just remember, be your best.
It matters only when you really try;
  Be your best, challenge that guy!
It is important to accept the game's test,
  But more important than winning—
Be your best.

BE A DREAMER

The first step toward success begins with a dream. There is nothing wrong with wanting to succeed as an athlete or, more important, as a person.

Many people dream dreams that may be fantasies, and they fail. It's all right to fail, but one should dream dreams that have the potential of becoming reality.

There is nothing wrong with dreaming of being the superstar or the M.V.P., except that for most of us, it is unattainable. But that dream may encourage us to reach *beyond* our wildest imagination to attain our maximum ability. For without the dream, we may fall short of our full potential—which just might mean being the M.V.P.

Happy are those who dream dreams and are ready to pay the price to make them come true.

—CARDINAL SUENENS

The biggest room in America is the room for improvement.

In the world of give and take, there are not enough people who are willing to give what it takes.

If you work—work hard.
　　If you play—play hard.
　　　　If you pray—pray hard.
　　　　　　Anything worth doing is worth doing well.

　　Sport consists of making right decisions.
　　So does Christianity.

The objective for the Christian athlete is to become the best child of God it is possible to be.

Therefore we also, since we are surrounded by so great a cloud of witnesses, let us lay aside every weight, and the sin which so easily ensnares us, and let us run with endurance the race that is set before us, looking unto Jesus.

—HEBREWS 12:1-2a NKJV

In a race, everyone runs but only one person gets first prize. So run your race to win. To win the contest you must deny yourselves many things that would keep you from doing your best. An athlete goes to all this trouble just to win a blue ribbon or a silver cup, but we do it for a heavenly reward that never disappears. So I run straight to the goal with purpose in every step. I fight to win. I'm not just shadow-boxing or playing around. Like an athlete I punish my body, treating it roughly, training it to do what it should, not what it wants to. Otherwise I fear that after enlisting others for the race, I myself might be declared unfit and ordered to stand aside.

—I CORINTHIANS 9:24-27 TLB

PAUL—the athlete:
    He was not a giant physically;
        he was a giant spiritually.

Bodily exercise is all right, but spiritual exercise is much more important and is a tonic for all you do. So exercise yourself spiritually and practice being a better Christian, because that will help you not only now in this life, but in the next life too.

—I TIMOTHY 4:8 TLB

Let God train you, for he is doing what any loving father does for his children.

—HEBREWS 12:7 TLB

God will meet our needs, but our wants may not be what God wanted for us. Therefore, we may want victory or stardom, but God only wants us to have a proper attitude about winning and stardom. Trying our best no matter what the outcome of the score; having a sincere, positive appreciation for our teammates and opponents; showing good sportsmanship; and adopting a strong positive attitude about competition —these may just be what we need—not what we want. Jesus will meet our every need—but maybe not our every want.

We must rise above ourselves; we have the ability to do it. The question remains—are we willing to do it?

"I am sure that God who began the good work within you will keep on helping you grow in his grace until his task within you is finally finished on that day when Jesus Christ returns" (Philippians 1:6 TLB).

All of us have special abilities God has given us. We must discover those abilities and pursue them to their fullest potential. But we must also be realistic and realize our limitations. We may desire to play one position, yet our abilities lie in another area. Discover your abilities—then go for it 100 percent!

"All our greatness is like a flower that droops and falls; but the Word of the Lord will last forever" (I Peter 1:24*b*-25*a* TLB).

"You need to keep on patiently doing God's will if you want him to do for you all that he has promised" (Hebrews 10:36 TLB).

PREGAME PREPARATION . . .
THINK ON THESE
THINGS

I am not bound to win,
But I am bound to be true.
I am not bound to succeed,
But I am bound to live up to what light I have.
I must stand with anybody that stands right;
Stand with him while he is right,
And part with him when he goes wrong.

—ABRAHAM LINCOLN

◊

Prayer

Lord, there's a game tonight! Of course I want our team to win, but even more than that, Lord, I want our team to do its best. I ask not for victory, but for honest effort on my part—and on the part of all our players, our coaches, our opponents, the fans, and the officials. Let the game be full of excitement as our teams vie for the prize of victory, but don't allow victory to overshadow our ability to do our best. May our witness for You be honorable. May others find in our spirit of competition and fair play the example of Jesus Christ, that he may be glorified. Allow us the strength and endurance to use our skills of play; grant that we may control our minds, bodies, and emotions; instill in us respect for our opponents and officials; protect us all from unworthiness, unfairness, and injury; and help us make this game one in which Christ shall be magnified and honored by our lives.

Thank you for this freedom to compete, in Jesus' name.

Amen.

Let love be your greatest aim.

—I CORINTHIANS 14:1*a* TLB

Now God gives us many kinds of special abilities, but it is the same Holy Spirit who is the source of them all. There are different kinds of service to God, but it is the same Lord we are serving. There are many ways in which God works in our lives, but it is the same God who does the work in and through all of us who are his. The Holy Spirit displays God's power through each of us as a means of helping the entire church.

—I CORINTHIANS 12:4-7 TLB

All the special gifts and powers from God will someday come to an end, but love goes on forever.

—I CORINTHIANS 13:8 TLB

Paraphrase of I Corinthians 12:12-31

Just as a team is a unit but has many players, and all the players on the team—even though there are many of them—make up one team, so it is with Christ. For by one Spirit we all were selected for this squad—whether Americans or Europeans, Caucasian or Negro—and all have been inspired by the one Spirit.

For the team does not consist of one player, but of many. If the guard should say, "Because I am not an end, I do not belong to the team," that would not make him any less a member of the team.

If the outfielder should say, "Because I am not a pitcher, I do not belong to the team," he would still be a necessary member of the team.

If the whole team were pitchers, who would cover third? If the whole team were halfbacks, who would snap the ball? But as it is, God has arranged the positions on the team, according to the rules of the game. If everybody played the same positions, where would the team be? So there are many positions, but only one team. The quarterback cannot say to the tackle, "Who needs you?" Nor the forward to the guard, "Get lost." On the contrary, the positions which may seem to be inconspicuous may really be indispensable.

Now you are a team for Christ. Each of you is a team member and God has assigned different positions to be played. So you are certainly wise to desire the finest skills. I will show you a more excellent way.

If I can play many sports well, but have not love, I am merely a flashy player.

If I know all about athletics and have the skill to become a coach, but have not love, I am just a nobody.

If I really give all I've got to being an outstanding player, but have not love, my score is zero.

Then what is love?

Love is a combination of many attitudes . . . like patience, kindness . . . like considering the other person's point of view . . . like not being glad when somebody drops out, but being glad when he makes good.

There are three basic skills for living: faith, hope, and love. But the greatest of these is love.

Reprinted by permission of the Fellowship of Christian Athletes from the September 1966 issue of its former national magazine, *The Christian Athlete*, now *Sharing the Victory*.

Love is very patient and kind, never jealous or envious . . . boastful or proud . . . haughty or selfish or rude. Love does not demand its own way. It is not irritable or touchy. It does not hold grudges and will hardly even notice when others do it wrong. It is never glad about injustice, but rejoices whenever truth wins out. If you love someone you will be loyal to him no matter what the cost. You will always believe in him, always expect the best of him, and always stand your ground in defending him.

—I CORINTHIANS 13:4-7 TLB

Someone said:
  Loving the game is great;
  Playing the game is greater;
  Winning the game is the greatest.

Someone else said:
  Winning the game is great;
  Playing the game is greater;
  Loving the game is the greatest.

I agree!

Four things a man must learn to do
If he would make his record true:
To think without confusion clearly;
To love his fellowmen sincerely;
To act from honest motives purely;
To trust in God and Heaven securely.

—HENRY VanDYKE

I *Am an Athlete*

I am an athlete!

I push myself to the point of pain so that I may endure in the race.

I practice my skills again and again until the boredom of repetition pushes my mind to its very limits, so that I may accomplish the task I have before me: to be my very best.

I learn to give my all, even to the point of giving up—then I give more, so that I may succeed.

I am an athlete.

I must do my best—through training, in practice, and in the contest—to give more than I believe I can, in order to fulfill my task.

I am an athlete!

I am a Christian athlete!

I push myself to the point of pain, remembering that Jesus went through untold pain for my salvation.

I practice my skills again and again to accomplish the task of the contest—yet I practice my Christianity continually—not to the point of boredom, but to the point of that inexpressible joy found only through Christ.

I learn to give my all, my best—not only in the contest, but in life; to live every moment fully—for Jesus gave his all upon Calvary's cross.

I am a Christian athlete. I practice my skills to do my best to win. And yet, I know the real champion of all life is Jesus Christ—and all I do is for his glory.

It is quite true that the way to live a godly life is not an easy matter. But the answer lies in Christ.

—I TIMOTHY 3:16a TLB

Don't worry about anything; instead, pray about everything; tell God your needs and don't forget to thank him for his answers. If you do this you will experience God's peace, which is far more wonderful than the human mind can understand. His peace will keep your thoughts and your hearts quiet and at rest as you trust in Christ Jesus.

—PHILIPPIANS 4:6-7 TLB

Always be joyful. Always keep on praying. No matter what happens, always be thankful, for this is God's will for you who belong to Christ Jesus.

—I THESSALONIANS 5:16-18 TLB

Obey God because you are his children; don't slip back into your old ways—doing evil because you knew no better. But be holy now in everything you do, just as the Lord is holy, who invited you to be his child.

—I PETER 1:14-15 TLB

The whole Bible was given to us by inspiration from
God and is useful to teach us
   what is true
     and
        to make us realize what is wrong in our lives;
           it straightens us out
                 and helps us do what is right.
At is God's way of making us well prepared
     at every point, fully equipped to do good to
        everyone.

—II TIMOTHY 3:16-17 TLB

Prepare me, Lord, for the game today.
  Help my endurance to last.
  Grant that my strength does not fail.
  Create the best through my skills.
  Control my temper at all times.
  Instill fairness in my competitive desire.
  Cleanse from my thoughts all that is
    unsportsmanlike.
  Make me an example for the younger
    players.
May my light shine as a beacon for all to see
    Jesus in my life.

My God will supply all that you need from his glorious
resources in Christ Jesus.

—PHILIPPIANS 4:19 Phillips

But they that wait upon the Lord shall renew
their strength;
they shall mount up with wings as eagles;
they shall run, and not be weary;
and they shall walk, and not faint.

—ISAIAH 40:31 KJV

WORDS OF ENCOURAGEMENT DURING THE GAME

Treat men exactly as you would like them to treat you. . . . Don't judge other people and you will not be judged yourselves. Don't condemn and you will not be condemned. Forgive others and people will forgive you. Give and men will give to you. . . . For whatever measure you use with other people, they will use in their dealings with you.

—LUKE 6:31, 37-38 Phillips

◇

EVER GET INTO A FIGHT?

"It is an honor for a man to stay out of a fight. Only fools insist on quarreling" (Proverbs 20:3 TLB).

Can tempers flair during a ballgame? You know they can. Anger is a human emotion we all have, but it needs to be controlled.

During a close game, it is easy for us to lose our tempers, and this often causes a fight.

Fans always seem to cheer when two ballplayers swing at each other. As Christians, we must learn to control ourselves.

It is a better person, and in reality one everyone admires, who controls emotions—exhibits sportsmanship—is fair in play.

Remember! It is an honor to stay out of a fight. It honors Christ. It honors the person.

"It is better to be slow-tempered than famous; it is better to have self-control than to control an army" (Proverbs 16:32 TLB).

For I want you always to see clearly the difference between right and wrong, and to be inwardly clean, no one being able to criticize you from now until our Lord returns.

—PHILIPPIANS 1:10 TLB

Remember! Your Christian conduct is as important on the field or court as it is off the field or court.

YE SHALL BE MY WITNESSES

Jesus commanded us as Christians to be his witnesses. This means that as athletes, we are to share our faith with others. Most people, athletic or not, enjoy hearing an athlete speak. As an athlete, doors of opportunity will open for you to speak for Christ.

In Luke 21:13, we read that we should take advantage of every opportunity to share our faith:

"It will turn out for you as an occasion for testimony" (NKJV).

"This will be your chance to witness for me" (Phillips).

"This will be your chance to tell the Good News" (TEV).

Remember that you represent a team or a particular sport, and you must represent that sport to the best of your ability. As followers of Jesus, we must represent him and share him with those who come to hear us speak or watch us play.

Now if you have known anything of Christ's encouragement and of his reassuring love; if you have known something of the fellowship of his Spirit, and of compassion and deep sympathy, do make my joy complete—live together in harmony, live together in love, as though you had only one mind and one spirit between you. Never act from motives of rivalry or personal vanity, but in humility think more of each other than you do of yourselves. None of you should think only of his own affairs, but consider other people's interests also. Let your attitude to life be that of Christ Jesus himself.

—PHILIPPIANS 2:1-5 Phillips

What we say is heard,
What we do is seen;
It may be kind,
It may be mean.

A simple poem that speaks about our influence.

One Solitary Life

He was born in a small village, the child of poor parents. He worked in a carpenter shop in another small village until he was thirty, shaping the native wood.

For three years he wandered as an itinerant preacher, never more than two hundred miles from his birthplace. He never attended college; he never wrote a book; he never commanded an army or painted a picture or built a monument or held an office.

While he was still young, his own people turned against him. His friends ran away, and one betrayed him for thirty pieces of silver. He went through the mockery of a trial, was condemned to death and nailed to a cross between two thieves. His body was placed in a borrowed tomb.

After almost two thousand years, no one has so touched human life. Today he is the center of the world's interest. Books on his life fill the libraries. His gospel covers the earth. His influence is the one sustaining hope of the future.

All the armies that ever marched, all the kings who ever reigned, all the governments that have risen and fallen have not affected lives upon this earth as greatly as has that *one solitary life*.

—AUTHOR UNKNOWN

The Value of Your Influence

We place value on many things, but have you ever placed a value on your influence? So often we look at outstanding coaches or players and place their worth pretty high or low, depending on how we value them. We often admire those of high value and wish we could attain such stature.

The answer is to discover who we are. God gave each of us unique abilities, and we should place a high value on those strengths. Be the person of value you are—the person of worth God created you to be. You may not be the number one player, but you have a valuable contribution to make. Discover and project your value. How much you value yourself just may be how much others value you.

TEAM INFLUENCE

Have you ever considered your team's influence on the conduct of your opponents? Let me share a beautiful story:

One basketball coach encouraged his players to respond to any foul called on them by the official with, "Good call!" And every time the official handed them a ball for a foul shot or an out-of-bounds play, they were to say "Thank you!"

This conduct sure changed the attitude of the officials, and good sportsmanship spread throughout the league.

Paul told young Timothy: "Do not let anyone look down on you because you are young, but be an example for the believers in your speech, your conduct, your love, faith, and purity" (I Timothy 4:12 TEV).

We are molded by others. Our character is influenced by those we meet or listen to. It is important that we, as Christians, are influenced by those who exhibit kindness, encouragement, goodness, concern, rightness. Everyone we meet becomes a part of us—either positively and negatively. So choose wisely those whom you look to as examples.

"And we know that all that happens to us is working for our good if we love God and are fitting into his plans" (Romans 8:28 TLB).

"Love knows no limit to its endurance, no end to its trust, no fading of its hope; it can outlast anything. Love never fails" (I Corinthians 13:7-8 Phillips).

It is not what you have done
Or what you may possess,
But what you are
That makes you a success.

SPORTSMANSHIP

"Sportsmanship is bringing out the best in play, attitude, and feelings."

"Sportsmanship is guiding the coach, player, team, and spectator to an attitude of fair play. It is observing all the rules, establishing appreciation for team members, opponents, and officials. It is having the ability to keep cool under all circumstances."

"The quality of a champion is found not just in victory, but in dedication toward that victory. A champion has that will to win, not just wanting to win; he has to be inspired in his efforts; he strives in each contest to give his best, no matter what the outcome; he takes God with him in all areas of life."

From Bob Sessoms, *The Volunteer Coach* (Nashville: Convention Press, 1978), pp. 18, 23. All rights reserved. Used by permission.

Happy are those who long to be just and good, for they shall be completely satisfied

—MATTHEW 5:6 TLB

Follow the Lord's rules for doing his work, just as an athlete either follows the rules or is disqualified and wins no prize.

—II TIMOTHY 2:5 TLB

To speak kindly does not hurt the tongue.

—A PROVERB

A true Christian athlete is one who, upon losing, does not sit and weep, but cheers the victor with the rest of the crowd.

Don't praise yourself; let others do it!

—PROVERBS 27:2 TLB

Read and Heed

It is far better not to say you'll do something than to say you will and then not do it.

—ECCLESIATES 5:5 TLB

And whatsoever ye do in word or deed, do all in the name of the Lord Jesus.

—COLOSSIANS 3:17 KJV

I will be careful about what I do and will not let my tongue make me sin.

—PSALM 39:1 TEV

Lord, who may abide in Your tabernacle?
Who may dwell in Your holy hill?
He who walks uprightly,
    And works righteousness,
    And speaks the truth in his heart;
He who does not backbite with his tongue,
    Nor does evil with his neighbor,
    Nor does he take up a reproach against his friend.

—PSALM 15:1-3 NKJV

*In Ephesians, Paul Offers Some Excellent
Guidelines on Sportsmanship:*

Be humble and gentle. Be patient with each other, making allowance for each other's faults because of your love (4:2 TLB).

Now your attitudes and thoughts must all be constantly changing for the better (4:23 TLB).

Stop lying to each other; tell the truth, for we are parts of each other and when we lie to each other we are hurting ourselves (4:25 TLB).

If you are angry, don't sin by nursing your grudge. Don't let the sun go down with you still angry—get over it quickly (4:26 TLB).

Do not use harmful words, but only helpful words, the kind that build up and provide what is needed, so that what you say will do good to those who hear you (4:29 TEV).

Quarreling, harsh words, and dislike of others should have no place in your lives. Instead, be kind to each other, tenderhearted, forgiving one another (4:31b-32a TLB).

Christians are not on the defensive—
we are on the offensive!

Success is a journey, not an event.

FEAR AND COURAGE

Years ago, President Franklin Delano Roosevelt spoke these words: "The only thing we have to fear is fear itself."

One of our problems as athletes is our lack of confidence. We fear failure; we fear the unknown; we fear our own ability to succeed. To overcome fear, we must step out in faith, do our very best, and take courage along.

It takes courage to line up in front of a 250-pound tackle; it takes courage to guard a 6'7" forward; it takes courage to pitch to a batter averaging .450; it takes courage to stand up before 5,000 fans and lead a cheer for a team that is behind 20 points with only two minutes to go.

It takes courage to do a great number of things. Why does it take courage? Because we fear. The Bible teaches us many things about overcoming fear:

"Be strong and of good courage, do not fear nor be afraid of them; for the LORD your God, He is the One who goes with you. He will not leave you nor forsake you" (Deuteronomy 31:6 NKJV).

"For God has not given us a spirit of fear, but of power and of love and of a sound mind. Therefore do not be ashamed of the testimony of our Lord" (II Timothy 1:7-8a NKJV).

"There is no fear in love; but perfect love casts out fear,

because fear involves torment. But he who fears has not been made perfect in love" (I John 4:18 NKJV).

"For you did not receive the spirit of bondage again to fear, but you received the Spirit of adoption by whom we cry out, 'Abba, Father' " (Romans 8:15 NKJV).

"So we may boldly say: 'The LORD is my helper; I will not fear. What can man do to me?' " (Hebrews 13:6 NKJV).

"Let him have all your worries and cares, for he is always thinking about you and watching everything that concerns you" (I Peter 5:7 TLB).

"God is our refuge and strength, a very present help in trouble. Therefore we will not fear" (Psalm 46:1-2a NKJV).

"Fear not, for I am with you. Do not be dismayed. I am your God. I will strengthen you; I will help you; I will uphold you with my victorious right hand" (Isaiah 41:10 TLB).

More Words About Courage

Wait on the Lord: be of good courage, and he shall strengthen thine heart; wait, I say, on the Lord.
—PSALM 27:14 KJV

I have told you all this so that in me you may find peace. In the world you will have trouble. But courage! The victory is mine; I have conquered the world.
—JOHN 16:33 NEB

But you, take courage! . . . For your work shall be rewarded.
—II CHRONICLES 15:7 RSV

Should you experience defeat, do not lose heart—this is the mark of courage.

It's so hard, Lord.
My teammates don't seem to care about you.
They call out your name profanely.
I've tried to be a witness to them,
   but they just laugh and make fun of me.
What's a Christian to do, Lord?

Whenever you feel discouraged, just turn it over to the Lord. He has promised to be with us and to help us. *Claim his promises!*

"Wait on the LORD: be of good courage, and he shall strengthen thine heart: Wait, I say, on the LORD" (Psalm 27:14 KJV).

"So, my dear brothers, since future victory is sure, be strong and steady, always abounding in the Lord's work, for you know that nothing you do for the Lord is ever wasted as it would be if there were no resurrection" (I Corinthians 15:58 TLB).

"Let us not grow tired of doing good, for, unless we throw in our hand, the ultimate harvest is assured. Let us then do good to all men as opportunity offers, especially to those who belong to the Christian household" (Galatians 6:9-10 Phillips).

Do You Feel Alone on the Team?

Do you feel alone on the team? Read this: "I will never, never fail you nor forsake you" (Hebrews 13:5b TLB).

Wow! That's God speaking. It's sometimes lonely to be a new member of the team, or the youngest member of a team, or at times when you just don't feel like a part of the team at all. Nobody really seems to care—even the coaches.

But with Christ in your heart, you can rejoice and just be yourself. Say to yourself, "In time, they will notice me. In time, they will see that my life's different; they will understand that I am a Christian. And I *will* make friends by just being myself and trying hard to honor Christ."

But don't try to be noticed for selfish reasons; don't try for self-gain. "You, like the lamp, must shed light among your fellows, so that, when they see the good you do, they may give praise to your Father in heaven" (Matthew 5:16 NEB).

We all want to be accepted, to be a member of the team. It may be that you are feeling a little down. Be of good cheer—have courage: "You will have courage because you will have hope" (Job 11:18 TLB).

"O my soul, don't be discouraged. Don't be upset. Expect God to act! For I know that I shall again have plenty of reason to praise him for all that he will do. He is my help! He is my God!" (Psalm 42:11 TLB).

Boy, I wouldn't be an official. No one really seems to appreciate the referees. But without them, the game would be a war. To express myself through sports, I must have freedom—

freedom to use my skills within the framework of the playing field;

freedom to give 100 percent within the bounderies of the rules of play;

freedom to strive to win the contest without infringing on another's right to play.

In order to have freedom, there must be an official.

Remember your leaders who have taught you the Word of God. Think of all the good that has come from their lives, and try to trust the Lord as they do.

—HEBREWS 13:7 TLB

Here I sit, Lord—
　　Not playing . . .

And, truly, I don't think I
really want to,
when the score is so close.

Commit everything you do to the Lord.
Trust him to help you do it and he will.
　　　　　　　　　　　　—PSALM 37:5 TLB

Why am I putting myself through all this, Lord?
I go out and work hard—for what?
I train, sacrifice, get chewed out, ignored.
FOR WHAT?

Fear not, for I am with you. Do not be dismayed. I am your God. I will strengthen you; I will help you; I will uphold you with my victorious right hand.

—ISAIAH 41:10 TLB

I was asked, "Why do you sit on the bench, game after game, knowing you probably will never play?"

I replied, "In order to advance my skills and strive to be the very best I can become—to be number one."

"But others are ahead of you and receiving all the fame."

I paused to think, then responded, "But I'm still having fun! Besides, the harder I try, the harder the guy ahead of me has to try, and he becomes better. As he tries harder and becomes better, the number-one player has to try harder and become better so as not to lose his position. I guess I am just helping him to be the best he can be."

Cling tightly to your faith in Christ and always keep your conscience clear, doing what you know is right.

—I TIMOTHY 1:19 TLB

I'm in a slump, Lord.
I can't seem to get my act together.
Coach wants me to try harder.
I just don't know what's wrong.
What should I do, Lord?

Take a new grip with your tired hands, stand firm on your shaky legs, and mark out a straight, smooth path for your feet so that those who follow you, though weak and lame, will not fall and hurt themselves, but become strong.

—HEBREWS 12:12-13 TLB

Maybe I'll lose,
but I'll lose trying.

AFTER-GAME
THOUGHTS

When the One Great Scorer comes
to write against your name—
He marks—not that you won or lost
—but how you played the game.
—GRANTLAND RICE

◇

Ever Experience Defeat?

Should defeat occur, remember that the other fellow, girl, team, or opponent just out-played you today. There will be another chance. Try harder to win. But more important than winning is remembering to do your very best. Contrary to popular opinion, it *is* how you play the game that counts.

It is better to attempt to play the game and lose than to just sit and watch. Some never enjoy playing because they fear defeat. Victory and defeat—both are part of the contest. Those who never try will never experience either—and that's sad.

Some Things About Defeat . . .

If you cannot win, make the one ahead of you break the record.

"There is no failure except in no longer trying."
—ELBERT HUBBARD

Worse than a quitter is the one who is afraid to begin.

"There are defeats more triumphant than victories."
—MONTAIGNE

It is far better to acknowledge failure and make a new beginning than to let pride bar the way to possible future success.

A person's aim may be higher than he or she is capable of achieving, but that person will go farther than those whose aim is low.

When defeat occurs, acknowledge it, learn from it, and start again. Don't be too proud to admit it; demonstrate that you can overcome it and succeed.

"Not failure, but low aim, is crime."
—JAMES RUSSELL LOWELL

Ever Feel Like Chucking It In?

Ever feel like chucking it in? Defeat is not the worst failure; not trying is the worst failure.

Ever get tired of sitting on the bench? Most of us usually end up there, and probably for these two reasons:

1. *We fear failure.* Yes, we are scared we will flub up, goof, make a stupid error and lose the game. As a bench warmer, it's only natural to feel that way.

AND

2. *We fear trying* because we might fail. There is an old saying: "He who has never failed is he who has never tried." A coach wants to see players try and try and try until they succeed. That's called *spirit*.

We need to overcome our fear of failure. In Galatians 6:4, the Bible tells us just to do our best. We can overcome our fears by turning them over to the Lord. Read on:

"I have the strength to face all conditions by the power that Christ gives me" (Philippians 4:13 TEV).

Or as another translator says: "For I can do everything God asks me to with the help of Christ who gives me the strength and power" (TLB).

Claim this promise. God may not make you the star, but he can take away those fears. He can instill confidence. You must believe he can—and he will. God is in the business of making winners out of losers. Don't just chuck it in! Go for it!

Far better it is to dare mighty things, to win glorious triumphs, even though checkered by failure, than to take rank with those poor spirits who neither enjoy much nor suffer much, because they live in the gray twilight that knows not victory nor defeat.

—THEODORE ROOSEVELT

I got angry tonight, Lord—
I hated that person so much.
You said we should love.
But not tonight, Lord.
I just couldn't love.

Above everything else be sure that you have a real
deep love for each other, remembering how love can
cover a multitude of sins.

—I PETER 4:8 Phillips

For this very reason do your best to add goodness to
your faith; to your goodness add knowledge; to your
knowledge add self-control; to your self-control add
endurance; to your endurance add godliness; to your
godliness add brotherly affection; and to your brotherly affection add love.

—II PETER 1:5-7 TEV

What the Bible Says About Anger

Now you must get rid of . . . anger, passion, and hateful feelings. No insults or obscene talk must ever come from your lips.

—COLOSSIANS 3:8 TEV

Be kind to each other, tenderhearted, forgiving one another, just as God has forgiven you because you belong to Christ.

—EPHESIANS 4:32 TLB

Man's temper is never the means of achieving God's true goodness.

—JAMES 1:20 Phillips

Don't be quick-tempered—that is being a fool

—ECCLESIASTES 7:9 TLB

Footprints

One night a man had a dream. He dreamed he was walking along the beach with the LORD. Across his mind flashed scenes from his life. In each scene, he noticed two sets of footprints in the sand; one belonged to him, and the other to the LORD.

When the last scene of his life flashed before him, he looked back at the footprints in the sand. He noticed that many times along the path of his life, there was only one set of footprints. He also noticed that this happened at the very lowest and saddest times in his life. This really bothered him, and he questioned the LORD about it.

"LORD, you said that once I decided to follow you, you'd walk with me all the way. But I notice that during the most troubled times in my life, there is only one set of footprints. I don't understand why, when I needed you most, you would leave me."

The LORD replied, "My precious, precious child, I love you and I would never leave you. During your times of trial and suffering, when you see only one set of footprints—it was then that I carried you."

—AUTHOR UNKNOWN

Playing the Game

So you played the game
    And you lost?
And you're battered and bleeding, too.
    And your hopes are dead
And you heart is lead
    And your whole world's sad and blue.
And you sob and cry
    In your grief and your pain
For the hopes that had to die.
    But the game is through
And it's up to you
    To laugh, though you want to cry.

For someone there must be to lose.
  It's sad but it's always true.
And day by day in the games you play
  It's sure sometimes to be you.
So grit your teeth to the pain,
  For you battled the best you could.
And there's never shame, in the losing game,
  When you lose like you really should.

For after all, life is a game,
  And we play it as best we may.
We win or lose as the gods may choose
  Who govern the games we play.
But whether we win or lose,
  At the end, when the battle's through,
We must wait with a smile
  For the after while
And the chance that will come anew.

                          —AUTHOR UNKNOWN

Some Words About Victory

The cheer rose from the crowd:

V - I - C - T - O - R - Y
Victory's our goal and that's no lie,
So look out, Bulldogs, we're hot tonight.
Come on, Raiders, let's *fight team fight*.

Victory—
—It's a word we all hear in athletics.
—It's the goal of competition.
—It's the prize for winning.

Victory—
—It's what the athlete trains for.
—It's overcoming an opponent.
—It's the opposite of defeat.

Victory—
—The fans expect it from us.
—The coach pushes us toward it.
—The thrill comes when we attain it.

Victory—
"So then, we must always aim at those
things that bring peace and . . . strengthen
one another" (Romans 14:19 TEV).

Victory—

"Don't just pretend that you love others: really love them. Hate what is wrong. Stand on the side of good. Love each other with brotherly affection and take delight in honoring each other" (Romans 12:9-10 TLB).

Victory—

"If we love God, we will do whatever he tells us to. And he has told us from the very first to love each other" (II John 1:6 TLB).

Victory—

"But thanks be to God, who gives us victory through our Lord Jesus Christ" (I Corinthians 15:57 NKJV).

WE RECEIVE THE VICTORY;
WE ENJOY THE VICTORY;
WE LIVE THE VICTORY;
WE MUST SHARE THE VICTORY.

The Athlete's Psalm

The Lord is my coach,
   I cannot lose.
He gets me in shape through drills in practice sessions,
   and makes sure I have a healthy training table.
He keeps me in condition:
He opens up the field for me to follow
   according to the boundaries and rules of the game
      so that I can be the Champion of His Cause.
Yes, even though the contest be on the brink of defeat
   I will not even consider the possibility of conceding,
      for
He always calls the right plays.
His discipline and direction (instruction and guidance)
   constantly challenge me.
He arouses my competitive spirit and
   inspires me to be at my best for the game,
      even though my opponent may have the home
         advantage.
He enables me to score even more points than I need.
I am confident that victory and triumph will be the
   result in the arena of my life, and
      when the final whistle blows,
         I will be enshrined in God's great Hall of Fame
         Forever.

                            —LARRY WALKER

Used by permission. Posters available from Vision, Box 544, Dallas, TX 75221

NIKE—(Nee'kay): Conquest; the means of success; victory

NIKOS—Conquer; overcome; prevail; be victorious

It is better to struggle for victory than to accept defeat.

Jesus promised that the Church would have the ultimate victory.

Thanks be to God who gives us the victory.

We are not talking about winning a ballgame or a contest; we are talking about victory over the powers of Satan. Jesus won for us the victory over Satan when he took upon himself the sins we have committed and will commit. We will win some of the battles against temptation and the devil, and we will lose some. But thanks be to God that through the death and resurrection of his only Son, Jesus, we have been given victory over the powers of darkness. It is a struggle for all believers to win over Satan, but we have already won; we have been victorious through Jesus Christ. By giving ourselves to him, we can claim that victory.

The Christian Has Already Won

A good friend of mine once said in a sermon: "The difference between an athletic race and the Christian race is that the Christian has already won."

In competition, victory is the goal we seek. We play to win. That's the object of the contest—to reach the goal of victory.

And so it is with life: We seek to win at living. This victory in life is discovered through faith in Jesus Christ, God's Son. Our opponent is Satan; the victory comes through overcoming Satan, who tries to destroy life.

In I John 5:3-5 (TEV), we read:

> For our love for God means that we obey his commands. And his commands are not too hard for us, because every child of God is able to defeat the world. And we win the victory over the world by means of our faith. Who can defeat the world? Only the person who believes that Jesus is the Son of God.

The victorious life for the Christian is found in complete surrender to God through Christ, who then has complete control. It is found in following the rules set by God for living; in applying the skills for living through daily study of the Bible and through soul-searching prayer; in practicing the discipline of obedience to his command to follow him and live a life of love.

It is our faith in Jesus Christ that gives us the power to claim victory and the power to defeat Satan. The Christian life is known as the victorious life. Only Christians can claim it; only Christians can share it. Share your victory!

Christians can live in confidence, for they have the victory in life, no matter what. They have the prize, the trophy, the title, the championship—for they have Christ.

"For God so loved the world, that he gave his only begotten Son, that whosoever believeth in him should not perish, but have everlasting life" (John 3:16 KJV).

In the game of life, the Christian has already won—ain't that great?

Ours is not to win the victory, for through Jesus, the victory is already won.

Overwhelming victory is ours through Christ who loved us enough to die for us.

ROMANS 8:37 TLB

"For God loved the world so much that he gave his only Son so that anyone who believes in him shall not perish but have eternal life" (John 3:16 TLB).

An athlete can have all the skill in the world, can be physically in shape, and can be a very good person morally, but miss the entire game. The Bible tells us that Jesus "increased in wisdom and stature, and in favour with God and man" (Luke 2:52 KJV). It is important to have a well-rounded life, as Jesus did, but most of us leave off the part about being in favor with God. We grow in wisdom through attaining knowledge in school and through sports; we grow in stature as we grow physically and train to make our bodies the very best in skill and conditioning; and we grow in favor with man as we grow socially by learning to get along with others. But we often do not measure up to the highest standards spiritually—in favor with God.

John 3:16 tells us that God loves us so much he gave his only Son, Jesus, to die for our sins. How can one become a follower of Jesus? A set of Scriptures found in the New Testament book of Romans tells us about this:

Romans 3:21-24 TLB

But now God has shown us a different way to heaven—not by "being good enough" and trying to keep his laws, but by a new way (though not new, really, for the Scriptures told about it long ago). Now God says he will accept and acquit us—declare us "not guilty"—if we trust Jesus Christ to take away our sins. And we all can be saved in this same way, by coming to Christ, no matter who we are or what we have been like. Yes, all have sinned; all fall short of God's glorious ideal; yet now God declares us "not guilty" of offending him if we trust in Jesus Christ, who in his kindness freely takes away our sins.

Romans 6:20-23 TLB

In those days when you were slaves of sin you didn't bother much with goodness. And what was the result? Evidently not good, since you are ashamed now even to think about those things you used to do, for all of them end in eternal doom. But now you are free from the power of sin and are slaves of God, and his benefits to you include holiness and everlasting life. For the wages of sin is death, but the free gift of God is eternal life through Jesus Christ our Lord.

Romans 5:6-11 TLB

When we were utterly helpless with no way of escape, Christ came at just the right time and died for us sinners who had no use for him. Even if we were good, we really wouldn't expect anyone to die for us, though, of course, that might be barely possible. But God showed his great love for us by sending Christ to die for us while we were still sinners. And since by his blood he did all this for us as sinners, how much more will he do for us now that he has declared us not guilty? Now he will save us from all of God's wrath to come. And since, when we were his enemies, we were brought back to God by the death of his Son, what blessings he must have for us now that we are his friends, and he is living within us!

Now we rejoice in our wonderful relationship with God—all because of what our Lord Jesus Christ has done in dying for our sins—making us friends of God.

Romans 10:8-13 TLB

For salvation that comes from trusting Christ —which is what we preach—is already within easy reach of each of us; in fact, it is as near as our own hearts and mouths. For if you tell others with your own mouth that Jesus Christ is your Lord, and believe in your own heart that God has raised him from the dead, you will be saved.

For it is by believing in his heart that a man becomes right with God; and with his mouth he tells others of his faith, confirming his salvation. For the Scriptures tell us that no one who believes in Christ will ever be disappointed. Jew and Gentile are the same in this respect: they all have the same Lord who generously gives his riches to all those who ask him for them. Anyone who calls upon the name of the Lord will be saved.

If you have not experienced Christ in your heart, if you feel you would like to know more about being a total person, if you would like to be a follower of Jesus, then all you have to do is believe those Bible passages. Just bow your head and, from your heart, ask Christ to come into your life and forgive you of your sins. You know what? He has already forgiven you before you ask, but you need to ask.

For more help in your new journey as a Christian, contact your Christian coach or a pastor of a church. Now that you have completed your decision to believe, then John 3:16 will mean everything to you, and grow even more meaningful each day as you walk the Christian journey.

THE ULTIMATE VICTORY

For whatsoever is born of God overcometh
the world: and this is the victory that
overcometh the world, even

OUR

FAITH

I JOHN 5:4 KJV